IMAGINE!
THOUGHT-PROVOKING POETRY

A WHISPER OF WORDS

Edited By Daisy Job

First published in Great Britain in 2021 by:

YoungWriters® Est. 1991

Young Writers
Remus House
Coltsfoot Drive
Peterborough
PE2 9BF
Telephone: 01733 890066
Website: www.youngwriters.co.uk

All Rights Reserved
Book Design by Ashley Janson
© Copyright Contributors 2021
Softback ISBN 978-1-80015-442-1

Printed and bound in the UK by BookPrintingUK
Website: www.bookprintinguk.com
YB0471H

FOREWORD

Since 1991, here at Young Writers we have celebrated the awesome power of creative writing, especially in young adults, where it can serve as a vital method of expressing their emotions and views about the world around them. In every poem we see the effort and thought that each pupil published in this book has put into their work and by creating this anthology we hope to encourage them further with the ultimate goal of sparking a life-long love of writing.

Our latest competition for secondary school students, Imagine, challenged young writers to delve into their imaginations to conjure up alternative worlds where anything is possible. We provided a range of speculative questions to inspire them from 'what if kids ruled the world?' to 'what if everyone was equal?' or they were free to use their own ideas. The result is this creative collection of poetry that imagines endless possibilities and explores the consequences both good and bad.

We encourage young writers to express themselves and address subjects that matter to them, which sometimes means writing about sensitive or contentious topics. If you have been affected by any issues raised in this book, details on where to find help can be found at www.youngwriters.co.uk/info/other/contact-lines

CONTENTS

Alleyne's Academy, Stone

Eloïse Rawsthorne-Durand (13)   1

Bartholomew School, Eynsham

Lydia Cleevely (12)	2
Ila Biggin (14)	4
Isabel Cleevely (12)	6
Isabella Marsh (12)	8
Beth Barton (11)	9

Blessed Hugh Faringdon Catholic School, Southcote

Izabella Mocarska (13)	10
Olivia Wojciechowska (12)	12
Dominik Woznicki (12)	14
Shantel Daniel Stafford (12)	15
Adrika Martins (11)	16
Aaditya Yadav (12)	17
Harrison Corp (11)	18
Nikola Jasman (11)	19
Oliwia Raczka (11)	20
Nina Zovko (13)	21
Jayda Charles (13)	22
Joshua Hugo (12)	23
Marcel Szadkowski	24
Nandini Jothi (12)	25
Flo Derrett (13)	26
Sanmitha Perera (12)	27
Brian Nyandoro (12)	28
Chioma-Eliora Nkwocha (13)	29
Charlotte Gulliver (11)	30
Cecilia Owino (12)	31
Gregory Cronje (11)	32
Enosh De Sousa (12)	34
Ethan Harding (13)	35
Michal Gorgon (12)	36
Freya Versace (12)	37
Jacob Grigg (12)	38
Kornelia Woznicka (11)	39
Demi-Louise Walters (11)	40
Olivia Bozetka (12)	41
Brandon Lyons (12)	42
Jakub Wollenberg (12)	43
Karina Czajka (13)	44
Thomas Conteh (13)	45
Natalia Kusak (12)	46
Oscar Hutchinson (12)	47
Szymon Berdak (12)	48
Maja Herman (12)	49
Sahar Ghaznavi (13)	50
Tristan Ashmore (11)	51
Nicola Kosmala (12)	52
Paulina Dusza (11)	53
Martin Ceperko (12)	54
Emmanuel Wireko Brimpong (11)	55
Joshua Mtetewaunga (11)	56
Mia Bartolone (12)	57
Khadija Sankoh (11)	58
Zofia Brettell (12)	59
Diana Amanullah (11)	60
Oliver Jones (12)	61
Divine Nnaji (12)	62
David Osei Kusi (12)	63
Dawid Zborowski	64
Kornelia Hryniewicz (12)	65
Gift Elihake (12)	66
Nora Otin-Jimenez (12)	67
Jack Trussell (12)	68

Jackson Hand (12)	69
Ayden Taveiro (12)	70
Beth McElligott (12)	71
Emily Aneke (11)	72
David Klampfer (12)	73
Ashlyen Lush (13)	74

Great Easton Primary School, Great Easton

T Rule (11)	75

Hylands School, Chelmsford

Emily Cross (13)	76
Jake Peters (11)	77
Thomas Easton (11)	78

Kingsbury School, Kingsbury

Harrison Fuller (12)	79
Holly Ruff (13)	80
Jack Homer (12)	81
Mia Braddow (12)	82
Gracie Matthews (13)	83
Lucas Humphrey (12)	84
Logan Lane (12)	85
Alexandra Simon-Zemanova (13)	86
Alice Mould (13)	87
Isaac Durbridge (13)	88
Sophie Clarkson (12)	89
Coel Garbett (13)	90
Lily Jackson (13)	91
Ben Hall (12)	92
Abigail Poole (12)	93
Charlotte Howard (12)	94
Rhianna Woolford (13)	95
Brandon Lewis (12)	96

Leyland St Mary's Catholic High School, Leyland

Aaron Lea (13)	97

Manchester Communication Academy, Harpurhey

Roxanne Parsons (13)	98
Jan Halas (13)	100

Oakwood School, Horley

Louise Gould (12)	101
Maddie Pelling (13)	102
Emily Vo (13)	104
Lucy Green (12)	106
Tejas Bhat (12)	108
Owen Dwyer (13)	110
Louis Greenall (13)	112
Lucy Duarte (13)	113
Sean Anyaogu (13)	114
Eldad-Leonard Soreata (12)	115
Abigail Killick (12)	116
Ayesha Zaman (13)	117
Jasmine Keane (13)	118
Oldriska Dickson (13)	119
Holly-Ruby Jackson (13)	120
Ellie-Marie Burchell (12)	121
Zara McKee (13)	122
Harry McMillan (13)	123
Daniel Youd (13)	124
Leah Pattemore (13)	125
Samuel Pannell (13)	126
Zara Tyson-Davies (13)	127
Alex Azoicai (13)	128
Cohen Masters (13)	129
Grace Clarke (13)	130
Lara Symonds (12)	131
Charlotte Crofts (12)	132
Connie Young (13)	133
Henry Duncan (13)	134
Sophia Dues (12)	135
Leah Branton (12)	136

Harley Greenhalgh (13) — 137

Rudheath Senior Academy, Rudheath

Luke Kierans (12) — 138
Melissa Coppock (11) — 139
Lewis Marshall (12) — 140
Erica Bowden (12) — 141
Miley Heath (11) — 142
Luke Wilkinson (12) — 143
Rhaghav Jevirajasingham (11) — 144
Bella Harrop Dobson (11) — 145
Dylan Lishman (11) — 146
Grace Foster (11) — 147
Max Kimber (12) — 148

Saint John Bosco College, Battersea

Mica Chaplin — 149
Taleigha-Shae Harris Hines (11) — 150
Barb Kostina (14) — 151
Luke Burt — 152
Rhiannon Pituc (11) — 153
Maluhky Stone — 154
Lorenzo Chetanneau — 155
Heryacos Habtamu — 156

St Ives School, Higher Tregenna

Isla Bea Ford (13) — 157
Evie Stattkus (13) — 158
Danielle Fox (13) — 160
Rowan Hodder (13) & Freya Baker (13) — 161
Fearne Slade (13) — 162
Esme Deacon (13) — 163
Ollie Trevorrow (12) — 164
Eva Fox (12) — 165
Ella-May Haile (11) — 166
Freya Scorer (12) — 167
Flossy Calder (11) — 168

St John Fisher Catholic College, Newcastle

Angela Manjooran (12) — 169

Waverley School, Bordesley Green East

Aishah Mallah (12) — 170
Ayman Ali (12) — 171
Aishah Saeed (12) — 172
Urooj Jamil (12) — 173
Rameesa Zamir (13) — 174
Habiba Feryad (12) — 175
Alisha Rahman (13) — 176
Sameera Yasmin (14) — 177
Hamna Iqbal (11) — 178
Haris Qadir (12) — 179
Abdullah Rashid (12) — 180
Huriyyah Shah (12) — 181
Aamilah Hussain (12) — 182
Kanz-Ul-Iman Choudhary (11) — 183
Malaika Muqaddas (14) — 184
Faisa Haybe (11) — 185
Maleehah Rahman (12) — 186
Mohammed Raheel (14) — 187
Farhan Hussain (11) — 188
Yahya Mir (13) — 189

Whitehorse Manor Junior School, Thornton Heath

Mia Wijesiri (10) — 190
Gabriella Danso (10) — 192

THE POEMS

One Leader, Two Worlds

Imagine the devil, a guru standing tall above the rest,
Out of reach,
No way to corrupt the corrupted,
The world crying out,
Imagine him taking away everything that keeps you breathing that keeps you alive,
You have no power you have no rights and you have nothing,
You're just something to mock,
No worth,
Nothing,
His path of destruction a wave so high it could never fall,
So many lies, so much corruption,
Blind to reality and what stares at you in the face,
Ignorant to what lies ahead,
Tricked,
Bemused,
The world crumbling beneath your feet, you will fall and nobody will be there to catch you,
Determination is the most powerful thing of all,
Experience before wisdom,
Believe me.

Eloïse Rawsthorne-Durand (13)
Alleyne's Academy, Stone

The 'Mind' Field

A prick of joy babbles and chats.
A wave of sadness holds you in its wrath,
The journey of wonder curls and coils.
An army of anger furies and boils.
A worry or fear can grow to a quiver.
The dagger of fright, a wink or shiver.
The needle of hope shattered and snapped.
Emotions, like glass, one slip and they're cracked.

Out on the plains happiness prances
Sadness plods and wisdom dances.
Noble steeds and glinting armour.
For every emotion brings with it more drama.
Protruding shields with bronze trinkets and trimmings.
Each day starts afresh with new emotional beginnings.
The sun emerges and the troops mobilise.
The silver moon retreats and puffy clouds wrap the skies.

They take their first shot, the arrow of revelation.
It brushes one's shoulder, a throbbing sensation.
Load! Aim! Fire! They howl.
A sudden gush of anger and a tingle of self-doubt.
They strike again, a stab of sorrow.
Though no blood is bled, just your heart is left hollow.
A tiny pearl tumbles down your cheek.
You lay awake at night. So content yet so weak.

Alas, the plucky horses are no more than faith,
The shields and armour protect you from fate,
The daggers and swords as they stab through your fears
The lionheart knights and valiant volunteers.
You shall always be curious and puzzled. Hence,
The Battle of Thoughts will always commence.
The penetrating insults are like the sting of a wasp.
The butterfly's wings flutter. The first taste of happiness that you ever got.

Lydia Cleevely (12)
Bartholomew School, Eynsham

Who Will You Be?

When will they go away?
Who knows what will happen?
They are still here today
Trapping you in a cabin

How are you managing
When you feel alone and you can't pursue?
Feeling like you are stuck where you are
No one to help you get through

Where will you be in a year?
How will you cope?
Will you still be here
Trying to get out of this mope?

When you're alone
No one there to help you get happier
Alone in your body
Standing there, with a barrier

What do you do
To try and help the stress?
How do you get through,
Get out of this mess?

No one sees the inside
They don't know what to do or how to help
They only see the outside
Not your mental health

But all of that could change in just one second
Talk to somebody about yourself
Don't make life a secret
Like a book on a shelf

Tell somebody how you feel
Make them aware of your emotions and how you're stressed
Don't leave them to figure it out
Do what is best

But you have to make the change
Feel positive
Feel like anything is in range
And be proactive

You might not want to let it go
But you can't keep it forever
So go on, do the right thing
It is now or never.

Ila Biggin (14)
Bartholomew School, Eynsham

My Place In Space

Spinning planets and shooting stars,
Ice-cold Neptune and flaming hot Mars.
Satellites zooming in our gravitational field.
I'm wondering what outer space could yield.

Sitting, waiting, wondering why?
Hours, days, weeks fly by.
A rocket dives through inky black,
Been going for weeks, there's no turning back.

But why am I here, what's there to see?
The sun and moon are not enough for me.
I want to know, where it all began,
Why we are here and who I am.

Years pass by, I still yearn to find,
The thing I've longed for all this time.
But out of the blue, my dream comes true,
A spiralling tunnel pulls me through.

Is this the end, is this what I desire?
I'm progressing up, higher and higher.
A flash of colours before my eyes,
I no longer see the dull, black skies.

On and on, it seems like hours,
Black holes whirling, meteor showers,
Venturing deep where satellites race,
Just imagine, what if we reached the edge of space?

Isabel Cleevely (12)
Bartholomew School, Eynsham

Would You?

Would you run into a burning fire to save the little girl?
Would you ride a horse backwards?
Would you stand up to the bully?

If your family was hanging onto their life,
If there was no hope left,
Would you hold their hand as they closed their eyes?

You sit silently in the dark alone,
They no longer sit with you in the dark,
Nowhere else to go.
Would you be someone else's light in their dark?

Would you sacrifice yourself for them to see the sunrise again?
Would you?

Isabella Marsh (12)
Bartholomew School, Eynsham

Wondrous Queen

Last night, I saw Queen
Keeping rhythm was Bass
Thunderous drums
Chanting guitar
Dancing, prancing Freddie

Screaming like lions
Fans worshipping idols
Clapping the beat
Sing loving harmony
Dancing, prancing Freddie

Flashing rainbow lights
Whirling, swirling mist
Snaking, sliding cables
Flashing, snapping cameras
Dancing, prancing Freddie.

Beth Barton (11)
Bartholomew School, Eynsham

Reality

Imagine your life just fell apart, you lost your job,
You lost your house, your only choice was to be outside,
But where could you go? There was no shelter,
Or any place to keep you warm, your only choice was the jagged pavements,
There was no other place you could stay at, you had no pillows,
Or blankets, just the plain cold,
You had to stay there, with your broken sign,
Saying 'please help', but it seemed invisible to everybody else,
You would spend most of your time there, waiting for help,
There was nowhere you could go, everything else looked the same,
You slept a few nights, you were weary,
You had to deal with it, there was no other choice,
Some people went past, giving you dirty looks,
But you didn't ask to live like this.
You got given the nickname 'homeless', is that a bad thing?
Then days passed, passed, there was still no change,
You were still alone in an empty street,
Your back started aching, your legs started to shiver,
There was no help, *maybe this was my fault,*
How did I end up like this?
Now the days were filled with nothing but rain,
All you heard was rain on repeat, it was like a lullaby,

But it got tiring, you had no shelter,
Your clothes were filthy, mostly wet,
It just got colder and colder,
As months went by, you were begging for help,
But nobody listened, nobody wants to listen to the homeless,
Some people went past, it gave you hope,
But all you got was a few coins, you should be grateful,
But you just want a friend, you don't want to be seen as filthy,
You want to be seen as 'normal', but people are scared of you,
You promise you're nice but nobody believes you,
You're still waiting for help, you still have that hope.

Izabella Mocarska (13)
Blessed Hugh Faringdon Catholic School, Southcote

Seasons

Summer, winter, spring, autumn,
Wind, sun, rain, blizzard,
Walking through whatever season,
Always there for no reason,
Summer, winter, spring, autumn.

Winter makes us hope for snow,
But the chance is very low.
Christmas at this time of year,
Hopefully it will make us cheer.

Spring, spring, joy outside,
Now there by your side.
Nature regrows, flowers pop out,
There will be an amount of fun!

Summer is finally here,
Get ready, it's time for cheer.
The beach is now welcoming us,
Come on, don't miss the bus!

Autumn is the orange time,
The clock is about to chime.
The year will end soon,
Time to look at that moon.

Summer, winter, spring, autumn,
Wind, sun, rain, blizzard,
Walking through whatever season,
Always there for no reason,
Summer, winter, spring, autumn.

Olivia Wojciechowska (12)
Blessed Hugh Faringdon Catholic School, Southcote

Outerspace

Imagine if we were in space,
And we controlled time,
We would play games and race,
Shining like stars, you and I,
Exploring everything beyond a hand's reach,
Uncovering treasure full of glory,
Planets, stars and universes we'd seek,
Swimming through like the fish named Dory,
But the darkness and sadness suddenly rose,
Nothing was fun, was it worth it anymore?
No matter if we discovered, nor did lovely art,
The isolation and this distance will tear us apart.
The world is so far away, would I even travel a light year?
The truth lurks within my heart, and I'll probably shed a tear...
But just think for a moment, at least we have a life
Things to do, learn and search, and an infinite amount of time
So go out there, have some joy, and play with your friends too!
And back at Earth, the human people will remember you.

Dominik Woznicki (12)
Blessed Hugh Faringdon Catholic School, Southcote

The Curse

What if immortality was a curse?
What if long life meant you felt every death was a part of you?
What if you could not age but scream in agony?
What if this time you felt the pain close?
What if you knew the pain as if it were a part of you?
What if it was your parent?
What if you felt them take their last breath?
Would you take the gift?
Would you take it? Would you?

Imagine if you lived forever at a price
Imagine if the price was to be Death's bride
Imagine if he treated you well but you felt the heat
Imagine if the heat was not from the strength of your love
But anger of the lost souls
Imagine if they hated you because you lived and they died
Imagine if they drifted like the wind in the sky
Imagine if you felt alone as even Death fled his bride
Would you still take the gift?
Would you take it? Would you?

Shantel Daniel Stafford (12)
Blessed Hugh Faringdon Catholic School, Southcote

The Day The World Changed

Something happened to the world today
A nasty bug called COVID came to stay
They told us to wash our hands and it might go away
But it was not enough to keep the bug at bay.

Lockdown was scary, it made me cry
I did not want anyone I know to die
School, shops and jobs were closed
At first, I gave a big woohoo!
But then we were told to stay at home
And soon I began to moan and groan.

Homeschooling started and my teacher tried their best to teach
But being with my family keeps me safe and well
But sometimes I feel like I'm living in a cell
An hour of exercise we are allowed every day
Sometimes it takes my sad feelings away.

We clap on Thursday for the NHS
To show them we know they are trying their best
Scientists are trying to find a cure
I am hoping for it soon but I am not so sure.

Adrika Martins (11)
Blessed Hugh Faringdon Catholic School, Southcote

Imagine We Were In ARK

I   would be punching trees for wood and thatch
F   inding a good place to build a base

W ater, water, I need water, I'm thirsty now!
E   scaping from a hungry raptor because I don't want to be lunch

W aiting for my dodo to get tamed, having a blast until I see an alpha raptor
E   ret, that's my castoroides (beaver), we are going to farm wood
R   ick is my doedicurus, me and him are best buds
E   dmond my dodo died from the alpha raptor, I'm gonna get my revenge

I   got my revenge and some sweet loot
N ow I'm really good at this game

A   RK is my new favourite game, so addictive
R   ex is about to be tamed next by me
K   iller is the rex's name because he wrecks everything.

Aaditya Yadav (12)
Blessed Hugh Faringdon Catholic School, Southcote

Imagine If

Imagine if I lived underwater,
Imagine if my life was a video game,
Imagine if I was immortal,
Imagine if I was the only one left in the universe,
Imagine if aliens took over Earth,
Imagine if I could time travel,
Imagine if I could fly,
Imagine if I could live on a different planet,
Imagine if I was an animal,
Imagine if there was another world war,
Imagine if my dream came true,
Imagine if I was stuck with bad luck,
Imagine if mythical creatures existed,
Imagine if magic was real,
Imagine if I was the richest person in the world,
Imagine if I was the poorest person in the world,
Imagine if I couldn't lie to anyone,
Imagine if I was stuck in prison,
Imagine if I won the poetry competition and won £100,
Imagine if lockdown was over.

Harrison Corp (11)
Blessed Hugh Faringdon Catholic School, Southcote

Monster Calling Morning

In the morning the streets were boring
All plain and orange, but I could still smell porridge
Though no one was cooking, the bowl was looking
All full and tasty, mmm, so amazing
The sun woke up, leaving the sky blue
Yawning, horning, the cars were moving
I still felt tired, even when the birds were tweeting
"Oh, I shouldn't have been up so late." Then a *bang bang!*
On the door, I went up the steps
Which were as creaky as the floor
The door was open, no one was there
All I could do was stare
Though I heard a creak upstairs
Was there someone actually there?
When I looked, I was took
And woke up in a dark space
"Similar to my room," I said
This was a dream overall, told me the
Monster... under... my... bed...

Nikola Jasman (11)
Blessed Hugh Faringdon Catholic School, Southcote

Perfect World

Imagine the world was perfect,
And no hearts would fall apart.
Imagine the world was perfect,
And we would be just like stars.
You see them shine together
To make the darkest night so bright.
But us, who are different people,
We shine and we make others dark.
The source, the luminous object is inside
And it's called a heart.

Imagine the world was perfect,
And no people would leave us because
The tears are worth more than a million pounds.

Imagine the brightest morning,
Standing together on front yards,
Smiling and dancing because
All of us shine so bright.
Imagine being yourself,
And having no mask,
That would be just perfect.
So let's make our world look like that!

Oliwia Raczka (11)
Blessed Hugh Faringdon Catholic School, Southcote

Revenge On The Evil

R est in peace, my dear relative
E nded her life for me in a car crash
V ery complicated relationship with him
E ven money matters more than love and life
N eglected us both until the very end
G reedy person who cared for nothing else
E njoyed the entire torture

O ccupied himself with our downfalls
N ever halted the traumatic game

T argeted us for the inheritance
H e achieved his goal, all he dreamed
E xamined the prices to know

E ven now I will prove the truth
V ying for our rights to justice
I 'm never going to give up
L oving pleasing revenge on the evil.

Nina Zovko (13)
Blessed Hugh Faringdon Catholic School, Southcote

Like They Said They Would

Imagine if I did speak up, would I be heard?
Would they actually listen like they actually care and listen,
Like they said they would?
Imagine if I actually told them who I was,
Would they still like me?
Would they still 'stick' with me,
Like I did to them?
Would they even be willing to do that for me,
Like they said they would?
Imagine if I told them why I can be so distant,
Would they still continue to talk about me behind my back?
Would they help me like they said they would?
Imagine if I woke up one day with the confidence to tell
them that they actually aren't nice people,
Would they invite me to their next sleepover,
Like they said they would?

Jayda Charles (13)
Blessed Hugh Faringdon Catholic School, Southcote

If I Won The World Cup

I can feel a raging fire in my heart,
The anthem running through my veins, ready to start.
So much is at stake,
I am doing it for my country's sake.
I hear the whistle, the crowd roar,
And yet I just want more.
This is real.
The clock strikes.
Ninety minutes, time is running out.
I have the ball,
I want to score, that's all!
I have a teammate calling for it,
No, a bigger fire in my soul has been lit.
It's alive, my heart is pumping,
I shoot, time stops,
Then all of a sudden, tick-tock goes the clock.
Goal!
With ice running through my veins,
A fire burning in my soul,
I've won the World Cup and made history.

Joshua Hugo (12)
Blessed Hugh Faringdon Catholic School, Southcote

My Life

Now I become a footballer,
I'm gonna be like Ronaldinho, a smooth skiller,
Everyone is gonna be calling me the GOAT,
And I'm going to have my own inspirational quote,
As I go through my football career,
There's going to be stress and fear,
I'm going to get a lot of criticism,
But rather than taking it personally, I'm gonna do the right decision,
I mean, I guess it's a part of a footballer's life,
Speaking about life,
As I will get older I'm going to have kids and a wife,
As my career comes to a close,
I hope they don't forget about me and I don't disappear like a ghost.

Marcel Szadkowski
Blessed Hugh Faringdon Catholic School, Southcote

We Are Not Alone

W hy do we think we're the only ones?
E ndless starts, galaxies way more than one,

A re we the only living things
R iding for each other's tiny rings?
E ven if we don't make it out,

N o time for melancholy, no time to pout,
O nly if it were true,
T he night's nebula portrays the clues,

A quamarine oceans glisten in the sun,
L ight above us making us want to run,
O nly if we knew what's there,
N eglecting this world could be more fair,
E ven though we're beautiful, we shall not compare!

Nandini Jothi (12)
Blessed Hugh Faringdon Catholic School, Southcote

Small World

Imagine if the world was small,
And not in a galaxy at all.
Imagine planets hung by string,
Arranged, dangling from someone's ceiling.
Imagine beings ten thousand times the size you've ever seen,
Their giant hands creating orbits that to them are just one swing.
Imagine us as pinprick dots,
And button-like countries that seem like spots.
Imagine space is just their air,
And there are hanging planets everywhere.
Imagine the problems that seem so big today,
Racism and sexism, one click of a mountainous finger and it would all go away.
Imagine if the world was small,
And not in a galaxy at all.

Flo Derrett (13)
Blessed Hugh Faringdon Catholic School, Southcote

No Freedom

Imagine if I were a shape-shifter,
It would be quite cool.
But on second thoughts this world can be quite cruel,
When you get something you want
And there's someone to take it from you.
Scientists chasing you, wanting to run tests,
Hunters hunting you, wanting your flesh.
Always in hiding, trying to blend in,
When really all you want to do is be yourself.
Everyone around you forcing you to fit in,
Influencing who you become when really
All you want is freedom.
This world is changing, but what exactly does this mean?
Freedom and friendship or inner sadness and captivity?

Sanmitha Perera (12)
Blessed Hugh Faringdon Catholic School, Southcote

Javier's Story

Imagine if you were in Javier's shoes.
His mum nearly died,
Don't test him.
His brother went out on a ride,
To find the suspects.
He got locked up trying to find them,
Javier's now got to not follow his brother.

Javier's going to find his mum,
He finds her on the bed dead.
He gets onto the floor, bawling,
Javier gets out his shank ready to take a life,
He finds the guys, he takes their lives,
Blood on his shirt,
Blood on his hands.
Oh, what has he done?
He hears the sirens.
Imagine, just imagine if you were in Javier's shoes...

Brian Nyandoro (12)
Blessed Hugh Faringdon Catholic School, Southcote

Come Back

Imagine us reunited
Alone, I was
Imagining your soft palms against my sorbet cheeks
Why do I feel such things?
Imagine you weren't so far away
Come back, come back
Imagining that I could see you eye to eye
Where are you?
As I sit on your grave imagining

My smile has faded
My lips have blisters
My health on the line
My energy, gone
Come back, come back
My love for you is everlasting
Do you feel the same?
You meant more to me than I meant to you
Now you're gone
As I sit on your grave imagining.

Come back, come back.

Chioma-Eliora Nkwocha (13)
Blessed Hugh Faringdon Catholic School, Southcote

Hiding Out Of Sight

Every night I wonder what if no one lived?
If no one walked on Earth?
If no one breathed the air?
If planets disappeared?
If there was nothing
But darkness everywhere?

Would there be nothing or something looming?
There, looming in the darkness of mystery and despair
Would there be spirits of people after life?
Would there be more planets hiding out of sight?

What if people lived in spaceships in the sky?
If we were green or orange and never died?
Or would there just be darkness?
Nothing in sight?
Nothing looming there, hiding out of sight.

Charlotte Gulliver (11)
Blessed Hugh Faringdon Catholic School, Southcote

BLM

B e better
L ove and never hate
A ccept everyone, no matter their skin colour
C are for black lives as well
K now that racism is wrong

L ives affected by trauma, violence, hate crime, racism
I magine if it all stopped
V alue each other
E verybody has the right to be respected
S upport the victims

M ake everyone feel welcome
A ttempt to stop racism forever
T each
T hink
E qual is what we should all be
R emember that racism is never okay.

Cecilia Owino (12)
Blessed Hugh Faringdon Catholic School, Southcote

Imagine If Aliens Existed

Imagine if aliens existed...
Would you...
Go to war?
Or make peace?

Imagine if aliens existed...
Would you...
Bring them in?
Or shoo them away?

Imagine if aliens existed...
Would you...
Be scared?
Or be happy?

Imagine if aliens existed...
Would you...
Try and communicate?
Or leave them alone?

Imagine if aliens existed...
Would you...
Ignore them?
Or help them?

Imagine if aliens existed...
Would you...
Hurt them?
Or protect them?

Imagine if aliens existed...

Gregory Cronje (11)
Blessed Hugh Faringdon Catholic School, Southcote

Demon King

The darkness rushed across the sky,
Terror filled the town with a cry,
People disappeared out of sight,
Nightmare spread on my face with might,
There was a person across the street,
Who looked like a silhouette,
Standing alone like your greatest nightmare,
Is it a dream or a terrible dare?
I was paralysed with fear,
Knowing that he would be near,
All I could do was scream,
But was it just a dream?
He appeared near me without a sight,
All he said was his name,
I woke up from a ring by my alarm,
On the wall it said 'Demon King'.

Enosh De Sousa (12)
Blessed Hugh Faringdon Catholic School, Southcote

My Last Day On Earth

Imagine if it was the last day of Earth
And nobody knew
Except for yourself,
So what would you do?
Would you warn other people
Or brace for impact?
Because this will happen,
That's a fact.
I would laugh with my family,
Spend time with my friends,
Clueless to the fact
That tomorrow is the world's end.
I would lie in a field,
Staring at the sky.
I'd appreciate the wildlife
As I say my goodbyes.
I'd look back at my life,
See how far I've come
As I watch the last ever setting sun.

Ethan Harding (13)
Blessed Hugh Faringdon Catholic School, Southcote

If I Were The Only Person On Earth

If I were the only person on Earth,
It would be great, free food, free water,
Free everything but no one to talk to,
Maybe a pet, but they can't talk or maybe,
An imaginary friend but no, they're just imaginary.

If I were the only person on Earth,
I could make my own TV show but,
No one would watch and anyway eventually,
Electricity would end, food would become old
And disgusting if no one would buy any.

If you have thoughts on being
The only person on Earth then don't,
Don't risk being alone.

Michal Gorgon (12)
Blessed Hugh Faringdon Catholic School, Southcote

True Feelings

Imagine if we didn't hide our emotions,
The scars were never there,
The masks had shattered the second they were made,
And the world didn't feel like slow motion.

Imagine if the words didn't cut that deep,
Butterflies didn't have to be drawn,
We didn't lie awake at night and cry ourselves to sleep.

Imagine if we didn't shake uncontrollably,
Panic in social situations,
Judge ourselves in the mirror,
Or starve ourselves continuously.

Just imagine if we showed our true feelings.

Freya Versace (12)
Blessed Hugh Faringdon Catholic School, Southcote

Time

Imagine pausing time, every second, every crime.
Having the power to have time to think about your decisions.
Escaping death with every breath.
Imagine getting away from anything.
Imagine saving people about to die, as you see the pain in their eye,
Saving them might rethink their life.
Pausing time can do a lot, saving every thought of every sort,
Maybe you'd use it on the basketball court,
Maybe to escape death and save your last breath,
Maybe you'd use it for crime, this is all in a matter of time.

Jacob Grigg (12)
Blessed Hugh Faringdon Catholic School, Southcote

Make A Wish

Imagine if you could fly,
Imagine if you could be strong,
Imagine if you could be invisible,
Imagine you could be super fast,
Then you would never be last!

Imagine you could be like Superman, Batman and Spider-Man,
Imagine you could be a superhero,
Just imagine.

Make a wish, make a wish,
In anything you can succeed,
To be an artist, archaeologist, teacher, footballer, basketballer,
Of anything you can be,
You just need to do one thing,
Make a wish and succeed.

Kornelia Woznicka (11)
Blessed Hugh Faringdon Catholic School, Southcote

By Her Side

What would happen if you woke up and your mum told you she had cancer?
Would you be sad, sorry or somehow mad?

Would you be sad because you would get no more hugs?
Or would you be mad because you'd get no toys?
Would you be by her bedside after she just had chemo?

She loses her hair bit by bit
Until there is nothing left
So you cut all your hair in support for her
For her birthday you give her the wig
That is made from your hair
And you say, "I love you, Mom!"

Demi-Louise Walters (11)
Blessed Hugh Faringdon Catholic School, Southcote

The Simple Truth

Imagine if you could only speak the truth,
The world would be different,
Very different,
Good and bad would happen,
Friends would come and go,
What would we become?
Saying all the things we have to say,
Instead of keeping them away,

But truthfulness is not always good,

Getting told that everything will be okay,
But no way will we stay with no pain,
Negativity, hopelessness, despair,
Are all part of the game,
The game of truth,
The one we all disobey.

Olivia Bozetka (12)
Blessed Hugh Faringdon Catholic School, Southcote

Imagine If Kids Ruled The World

If kids rule the world
There will be no more chores
And now your parents are now scrubbing the floor.
You can now sit on the couch
And watch your parents pout.

You get to sleep in
And don't have to take out the bin.
And go on your phone all day
And see your parents give you your food on a tray.

And you can go to sleep late
And in the morning get your breakfast on a silver plate.
And go and play your games
And give your parents silly names.

Brandon Lyons (12)
Blessed Hugh Faringdon Catholic School, Southcote

Liking It

I wonder, some car,
Imagining something,
Liking, wishing,
Too bad, too expensive...
But it looks fierce like an eagle.

3, 2, 1... go!

I just want to like it!
Everybody stoppin'!
Wishing this dream could come true!
But it's highly unlikely...
Keep pushing forward!

OG... 1, 2, 3

Well, it's over, hope is lost,
People are right, it's bad,
I will go like another car...
But I won't stop liking it.

Jakub Wollenberg (12)
Blessed Hugh Faringdon Catholic School, Southcote

Black And White

All so lovely, then so lonely,
The fear is seeking,
For my mind to haunt me.
It went so silent, it went so dull,
Was so quiet, think I'm losing it all.
I look in the mirror, what can I see?
Someone who's lost in an endless dream.
It's been so quiet, where is the past?
Why do I see a future me?
Crying in bed, still feeling dead,
Will it end if I find the left?
Of a better me, at once so free,
Just as in the past, that I cannot trust.

Karina Czajka (13)
Blessed Hugh Faringdon Catholic School, Southcote

Imagine If Kids Could Rule

Imagine if kids could rule,
That would be so cool.
We would go on planes and ride first-class flights,
Play games all day and tell the adults what's right.
We would tell the teachers when to speak,
There would be no school all week.
We would drink fizzy drinks all day,
And when we are at our cousin's we decide how long we stay.
We would go to McDonald's and order 10,000 Happy Meals,
And when you get it you will think *is this all real?*

Thomas Conteh (13)
Blessed Hugh Faringdon Catholic School, Southcote

Imagine If I Lived Underwater

If I lived underwater,
I would feel free,
If I lived underwater,
I would build a kingdom.

If I lived underwater,
I wouldn't burn in the sun,
If I lived underwater,
I would take you with me.

If we lived underwater,
We would have a blast,
If we lived underwater,
We would have a sleepover every night.

If we lived underwater,
We could invite our friends,
If we lived underwater,
The fun would never end.

Natalia Kusak (12)
Blessed Hugh Faringdon Catholic School, Southcote

Global Warming

The junk fills the streets
Every day when you sleep
Over, over and over
Worse, worse, worse
I try not to think
How bad it could be
And when the ash fills the sky
And all the animals die
We will regret it, don't lie
But what if it was not like this?
Everything could be better
Trees and leaves could be all around
Not bottle caps and glass on the ground
If it was this it would be better
I wish the world could be fresher.

Oscar Hutchinson (12)
Blessed Hugh Faringdon Catholic School, Southcote

Life?

Imagine we were all immortal, would we be living?
What would be the point of life?
Imagine if we were in a simulation and nothing we would do would matter.
Imagine if animals ruled the Earth, what could they do?
Imagine if everyone was a clone, would anything matter?
Does anything matter?
Imagine if there were many other life forms in our solar system.
Imagine if in our life one of the many planets had different types of people and different Earths.

Szymon Berdak (12)
Blessed Hugh Faringdon Catholic School, Southcote

The Truth

Imagine if they knew what you think about
Come up to ask you if you're okay
But all you think about is doubt
It's like they're asking for the wrong way
You answer with a classic response
So they walk away like you're invisible
You are living in a world of lies
Thinking that everyone is responsible
But instead you ignore every one of your tries
To at least think the same as them
Instead of getting away with murder.

Maja Herman (12)
Blessed Hugh Faringdon Catholic School, Southcote

What My Future Holds

In the future, I want to be rich,
In the future, I need to be rich,
For the future, I wish to be happy,
But I do not wish to be scrappy.
Always have hope in what the future holds,
Never lose hope or it folds.
Life is only given once,
So do everything your heart desires,
You don't know when your death lies.
Always follow your dream.
In life, always gleam,
Life is like a stream,
Always flowing but coming to an end...

Sahar Ghaznavi (13)
Blessed Hugh Faringdon Catholic School, Southcote

Imagination

Imagine you were a superhero.
Imagine you were who you wanted to be!
Imagine you could rule the world.
Imagine you could have all the power!
Imagine going to Mars.
Imagine going where you desire to go!
Imagine being a villain.
Imagine being someone you didn't want to be!
Imagine bringing the world peace.
Imagine being one of the greats!
Imagine doing what you want for life!
Your imagination can run wild.
So let it!

Tristan Ashmore (11)
Blessed Hugh Faringdon Catholic School, Southcote

True Happiness

True happiness,
No violence, no ambulance around,
No millions seeking help,
No creeping in the woods.

True happiness,
No people protesting, just many resting,
None begging, none stressing,
Though forgetting the past.

True happiness,
Many smiling and surviving
The present today,
Just pleasant walks around the park,
Nothing lurking, hidden in the dark,
Though many celebrating their rights and cries!

Nicola Kosmala (12)
Blessed Hugh Faringdon Catholic School, Southcote

Imagine

Imagine if you had superpowers,
Stronger than ever, easy to control like a feather.
Imagine you ruling the world,
Doing whatever you thought.
Imagine living in space,
Flying and having a race.

Imagine there is no fight, no war,
You have family, health and you don't need more.
Imagine time travelling, changing history,
Revealing the mystery.
Imagine pausing time,
Writing poems, making it rhyme.
Imagine...

Paulina Dusza (11)
Blessed Hugh Faringdon Catholic School, Southcote

The Problem With Time Travelling

T ime travelling
I s a
M ystery to
E scape the devastating

T rouble of the
R uthless police that will
A rrive, not
V isit but
E nter your house and will make you
L ie down on the floor and no
L uck will save you this time
I f you somehow run away, they will still
N avigate themselves to you and will
G et you to jail...

Martin Ceperko (12)
Blessed Hugh Faringdon Catholic School, Southcote

Imagine You Have Powers

Imagine you have powers
I will fly to the sun
Run faster than anything on Earth
Be stronger than anything or anyone
Imagine you have powers
I will make the world upside down
Spend my holiday on any planet I want
Read anyone's mind and feelings
Make my dreams come true
Imagine you have powers
I will go to any galaxy I want
Teleport to any place I want
Imagine you have powers
Just imagine.

Emmanuel Wireko Brimpong (11)
Blessed Hugh Faringdon Catholic School, Southcote

It's Not Just A Game!

It's not just a game

It's life, it's a hobby, it's a habit
It's everything

It's not just a game

When you're on the ball you're going to have anxiety
You're going to be concerned
But that moment when you strike the ball and score a goal
You're filled with joy and happiness
Your team is filled with joy and happiness

It's not just a game.

Joshua Mtetewaunga (11)
Blessed Hugh Faringdon Catholic School, Southcote

Imagine If You Were Immortal

Imagine if the world ended,
Imagine if you were immortal,
If you were the last one alive...

Floating through the air,
Except with no air,
Being on your last breath
Every time you breathe,

Having no heart
But a heartbeat,
Being alive
But with no heat,

Not having friends,
Not having family,
When once you did...
Only having thoughts, memory,
Dreams.

Mia Bartolone (12)
Blessed Hugh Faringdon Catholic School, Southcote

Imagine Fame

Imagine if we woke up being the person we always wanted to be
Imagine if I woke up being a famous footballer
Like Christiano Ronaldo or Lionel Messi or even Marcus Rashford
Imagine, just imagine

Imagine if I woke up as a famous TikToker
Like Charli D'Amelio or Addison Rae
Imagine, just imagine

Imagine if I woke up as a rapper
Like Cardi B or Nicki Minaj
Imagine, just imagine.

Khadija Sankoh (11)
Blessed Hugh Faringdon Catholic School, Southcote

Pirate

Imagine if I were a famous pirate,
The crew would be loud and the sea silent.
My mates would be Barbosa and Sparrow,
Getting away with crime but only by narrow.
Drinking bottles of rum in the moonlight,
But by day, with swords, we'd fight.
We'd visit unknown land,
Bathe in water, tan in sand.
Last but not least I'd ride the Black Pearl,
The first captain ever to be a girl!

Zofia Brettell (12)
Blessed Hugh Faringdon Catholic School, Southcote

Lockdown

L ocked up at home, now I've got nothing to do
O utside of my house, clapping for the NHS
C OVID tests on the loose
K ids back into school wearing masks which is something new
D own below we're all worried
O nline school was a fuss
W hen this has all ended I'm going to a party
N ow this COVID-19, you say, has changed my life.

Diana Amanullah (11)
Blessed Hugh Faringdon Catholic School, Southcote

The Wall Calls

I magine if we could live forever,
N ot knowing the weather,

T here are people crying in the walls,
H atred is all that rules,
E nergy is slowly lost...

W ailing coming from the walls
A nimals fed to them all, the wall calls
L ess of the wall's calls!
L ess people calling,
S ay goodnight...

Oliver Jones (12)
Blessed Hugh Faringdon Catholic School, Southcote

Black And White

A world of black and white is a world made out of night
A world where the sun doesn't shine
A world that is not fine
A world with no escape
A world where some sleep in fright
A world of black and white
A world of endless hate
A world with black as bait
A world where some are squeezed tight
A world where black has no might
A world of black and white.

Divine Nnaji (12)
Blessed Hugh Faringdon Catholic School, Southcote

Imagine Being In A Video Game

Imagine being in a world where monsters are real
Imagine slicing and dicing to victory
Imagine being able to explore the world
Imagine winning a Victory Royale
Imagine having an everlasting bond with friends
If you could only imagine for a second
Imagine taking over the world
Even imagining makes it feel like a wild fantasy
But all you can do is imagine.

David Osei Kusi (12)
Blessed Hugh Faringdon Catholic School, Southcote

Imagine If

I magine if you had one wish
M aybe you would want to be rich?
A new house or 100 pounds and a...
G old trophy
I magine if every dream turned real
N ever doubt that though
E ven if your plans failed

I magine being that
F ootball player, gymnast or zookeeper.

Dawid Zborowski
Blessed Hugh Faringdon Catholic School, Southcote

Imagine Monday

I magine having to go to school on Sunday
M ondays are tiring
A pple in the morning and off you go to school
"G ood morning," the teacher says each morning
I f the teacher could be sick every day
N obody likes school on a Monday
E ventually, Mondays will have to be cancelled!

Kornelia Hryniewicz (12)
Blessed Hugh Faringdon Catholic School, Southcote

Imagine You're Me

Imagine you're me
Imagine phones disappeared

Imagine the world disappeared
Imagine your house disappeared
Imagine aliens came to your house
Imagine our schools disappeared
Imagine our friends disappeared

If my friend disappeared I would be alone
If my house disappeared where would I live?

Gift Elihake (12)
Blessed Hugh Faringdon Catholic School, Southcote

Imagine Being Born Twice

Imagine being born twice,
It's just like rolling a dice,
Leaving all the past behind,
And starting a new life!

Seeing all your family and friends,
But then, once again, it all ends,
It starts to flare up in my face,
But my next move is in ace.

Imagine being born twice.

Nora Otin-Jimenez (12)
Blessed Hugh Faringdon Catholic School, Southcote

Mandalorian

M andalore
A rmour made of Beskar
N ever-ending wars
D ark Troopers
A lways ready for a fight
L uke Skywalker
O verprotected
R azor crest
I G-11
A mban phase-pulse blaster
N ever surrendering.

Jack Trussell (12)
Blessed Hugh Faringdon Catholic School, Southcote

Life As A Homeless Person

Just imagine how life could have been
As I just sit on the street
Cold, shivering at night
Killing time by watching the dark, frightening sky
Sobbing and crying every hour of the day
Only wishing to find a place to stay
Nice to meet you, have a wonderful day!

Jackson Hand (12)
Blessed Hugh Faringdon Catholic School, Southcote

Space

S pace is a place where there is infinite space
P eople go there to explore and wonder how things work
A stronauts go up there to find new planets
C old as a freezer
E ndless imagination can be filled with space.

Ayden Taveiro (12)
Blessed Hugh Faringdon Catholic School, Southcote

In The Darkness

As I stood there in the dark
There was a noise from the park
Whoosh went the wind
Drop went a pin
A shiver went down my spine
All the trees were entwined
As I stood there all alone
In the darkness of the woods.

Beth McElligott (12)
Blessed Hugh Faringdon Catholic School, Southcote

The Night

The night sky, watching the night sky
The wind howling, the stars shining, lighting up the black sky
The 24-hour shop shining like a star
Small silhouettes sneakily moving
The trees swaying, the grass dancing, shining in the moon.

Emily Aneke (11)
Blessed Hugh Faringdon Catholic School, Southcote

Don't Call Me David, Call Me Dave

My name is David,
But you can call me Dave,
I go for a walk every day,
Here's a fun fact, I walk with my friends,
But all they talk about is the weirdest trends.

David Klampfer (12)
Blessed Hugh Faringdon Catholic School, Southcote

Imagine If Everyone Was Equal

A world free of pain
Where everyone isn't the same
And people don't have to change
There is no need to blame
A world free of pain.

Ashlyen Lush (13)
Blessed Hugh Faringdon Catholic School, Southcote

The Invisible Mythical Creature

I found a button in a bird box and pressed it.
It opened up a secret hidden wood, it was magical!
Suddenly, I questioned myself: should I go in?
Wow! What a sight!
There were rainbow-coloured trees, glitter for rain and a rainbow for the sun.
Suddenly, I caught a glimpse of a unicorn out of the corner of my eye.
Was it invisible?
I got a message and it said 10:30 still, I had been in the forest for over an hour.
Was this so magical that time didn't pass by?
I was sad to say that my adventure was over.

T Rule (11)
Great Easton Primary School, Great Easton

Sacrifice

I form my own fantastical view
A view I imagine the world should be
What if there was no pain? No war? No suffering?
What if we could be who we wanted to be?
Deep down whom we truly are
Pain destroys me when that thought comes through
Why do we criticize ourselves?
Even for just one day
There was no suffering
No pain
No war

I dreamed I was back at home
I dreamed I was with my family again
The only thought that ran through my blood
Through my skin, 'will I see my children again?'

The trenches were appalling
The shelling still not gone from my mind
This is my duty, my life
'It's all about sacrifice' they say.

Emily Cross (13)
Hylands School, Chelmsford

If I Ruled The Galaxy...

If I ruled the galaxy...
I would make everything anti-gravity.
I would float around like a balloon,
and make a zoo full of baboons.
I would play video games and eat ice cream,
all day,
that's my dream!
If I ruled the whole of space,
I would carve a planet with my face;
and above all,
even over my rule,
I would spend time with my friends,
once we've finished school.
If I ruled the galaxy,
I would eat a lot of sweeties!

Jake Peters (11)
Hylands School, Chelmsford

The Superhero

T hey fly across the sky
H e or she saves lives
E very citizen saved

S peed
U ltra vision
P sychic beams
E lectric fingers
R age strength
H e or she has all these powers
E very pow big or small
R eady or not
O f all the people the doctors are the closest we have got to a superhero.

Thomas Easton (11)
Hylands School, Chelmsford

Imagine If You Were Immortal

Imagine if you were immortal
Watching everybody around you pass
Eventually the world explodes
But you have a long time until that

Imagine if you were immortal
Time to change the world
You could heal the world's problems like a doctor
Time to travel the world
Have all the time on the clock

Imagine if you were immortal
Could watch trees dance until they were chopped
However, the world would become a bad place
A lot of animals could cease to exist
You would have to witness many injustices
Watch society crumble
Then after all the pain and suffering
Maybe being immortal wouldn't be such a great idea.

Harrison Fuller (12)
Kingsbury School, Kingsbury

Animals And Madness

What is going on? Am I going mad?
Is my head in a fuzzle? Is my brain too tired to function?
Even if I was mad, surely I would be glad,
For how is that mouse talking to me?
How am I talking to that donkey, chicken and llama?
To the horse, crocodile and flea?
For how is it possible to ribbit with a frog?
To meow with a cat, to honk with a goose?
To hiss with a snake, to bark with a dog?
All of this is impossible, it must be a trick,
Evilly played by my friends,
Played by Sophie or Susan or John or Nick,
Something is definitely wrong, I just want it to end,
Maybe I truly am going round the bend!

Holly Ruff (13)
Kingsbury School, Kingsbury

Imagine If Your Pet Could Talk

"Take me for a walk!" he said with a yelp
"Play with me forever, night and day!
When I'm locked in a cage I want to call for help
So unlock my cage and give me a hug
When my owner isn't here
I have the house to myself
I open up the fridge and steal a beer
Along with all the crisps on the shelf
Woof! Woof! now means hello
Oh I love my bone and ball
Let's go out in the snow
When there is a knock on the door I want to see them
So I run down the hall!"

They may not eat with a knife and fork
But imagine if your pet could talk!

Jack Homer (12)
Kingsbury School, Kingsbury

Life

Imagine if you were the last person on Earth
You start to look around and question your worth
Imagine if you could pause time
You could do anything you want, you could commit a crime
Imagine if you could change history
Nothing is the same as it used to be

Imagine if everything was equal
Everyone on the street seen as normal people
You can imagine anything
You could be a bus, a dog or even a sink
You could have a superpower no one has ever heard of
Anyone can imagine it's a part of life
But sometimes reality can stab you in the back with a knife.

Mia Braddow (12)
Kingsbury School, Kingsbury

Time Travelling

Imagine if you could time travel,
Fix the past to better the present,
Fly to Dubai and watch the sun dazzle,
No more using antidepressants,
Maybe I could be more joyful,
Go back to when I had no troubles,
When things used to be more humble,
My fear of the past returning like bubbles.
Imagine if you could time travel,
Look in the mirror and say everything is okay,
Be a good kid then Mother wouldn't cavil,
Take my sister out to play,
Maybe she wouldn't have been hurting,
Maybe then the police sirens wouldn't be alerting!

Gracie Matthews (13)
Kingsbury School, Kingsbury

Changing Timelines

Now my child, listen for a second more
What if you could alter the past?
Would you go back and pass a new law
Or would you try and achieve world peace?
Or would you try and take the holy land?
Or would you assassinate Joseph Stalin?
Would you fight Napoleon on land?
Or perhaps you could save the Hindenburg Zeppelin?
Maybe you could restore the British Empire
Would you try and stop slavery?
Personally I would join the cavalry
As they charge against the Novgorod line
But staying here in the present for me sounds fine!

Lucas Humphrey (12)
Kingsbury School, Kingsbury

I Am Alone

Nobody is to be found,
I am all alone,
No matter where I went,
I am alone,
Stuck scrambling for my life,
Scavenging around for food and water,
Travelling far from my home,
Crossing through all the places I see,
And yet I am still alone,
The air so fresh,
No pollution in the air,
The land is dying,
Structures are crumbling,
All because I'm alone,
I'm exhausted living like this,
My body is aching with pain,
My only option is to die.

Logan Lane (12)
Kingsbury School, Kingsbury

If The World Could Feel

Imagine if the world could feel
Sense our emotions and our touches
Oh, how its pain would then be real
Our planet would then need crutches
To experience the catastrophes
And empathise our loves
To feel the energy of 100 coffees
Or the joy of warm new gloves
Would it look at us in awe
When we made new discoveries?
And beam at the crow's caw
When it thought of its past memories?
Imagine if the world could feel
I wonder if its heart would heal.

Alexandra Simon-Zemanova (13)
Kingsbury School, Kingsbury

Imagine A Toy Came To Life...

A boy,
Brought in a toy,
To the terrible school,
It was an astronaut,
Who could fly high into the sky,
As he went up in the sky he waved goodbye.

The boy watched him,
He gasped in shock,
"I never knew he could fly!"
Up, up and jump!
The astronaut landed,
And said hi.

Up, up and jump
He dumped as quick as a bullet
"My name is Buzz Lightyear!"
The boy froze
As he itched his nose.

Alice Mould (13)
Kingsbury School, Kingsbury

Last One

The last person on Earth
What happened to the others is unclear
Everywhere is as quiet as a mouse
Nobody is in their house
Silence creeps around me as I remember
I am the last person on Earth.

I begin to wonder why
Did everyone just die?
What do I do?
How will I get my food?
I question my worth
As the last person on Earth
I can't survive
On my own
As the last person on Earth.

Isaac Durbridge (13)
Kingsbury School, Kingsbury

Reflection

A person behind non-existent glass
Is a mirror what I see?
I see a petal fall to the grass
Revealing a person right in front of me
The realisation hits me as sharp as a sword,
That under the cherry tree
Reaching forward
Is an identical version of me
Is this a dream?
Some sort of fantasy?
Though that is what it may seem
No mirror do I see
I stare back
At the girl with a blue backpack.

Sophie Clarkson (12)
Kingsbury School, Kingsbury

Imagine, Imagine, Imagine

Imagine if you were the last person on Earth
How amazing would that be?
So peaceful and calm
Not a single worry
Imagine, imagine, imagine
Imagine if you could change history
We wouldn't be where we are
The world would be a greater place
Imagine, imagine, imagine
Imagine if you were homeless
You would be all alone on the streets
You would be as cold as ice
Imagine, imagine, imagine.

Coel Garbett (13)
Kingsbury School, Kingsbury

Imagine If I Were Prime Minister

Everyone would eat sweets all day
Everyone would abide
Go to the park and play
And on their way we could have an animal to ride
We could dance as much as we liked
We could sing songs that rhymed
We could even have a bike ride
We would have fun for the rest of time
Nobody would moan or whine
The world would be healthy and clean
We would all get along fine
And nobody would be mean!

Lily Jackson (13)
Kingsbury School, Kingsbury

If Your Dreams Came True

Stay at home
Wear a mask
It is not very safe!
COVID-19 is killing the world
It's not very safe
You might be ill
You might be sick after lockdown
Your teachers won't miss a trick
We're back at school
Shops are opening
It's all normal
It's getting better
It's getting good
Imagine all your dreams coming true
Imagine COVID-19 was never a thing.

Ben Hall (12)
Kingsbury School, Kingsbury

If Only Objects Could Speak

Imagine if objects could speak...
Fruit and veg,
Candles, chairs and leeks,
Even the bakery called Greggs,
Including shoes and coats,
Imagine if animals could speak...
Animals such as goats,
White boards and walls,
Paper and pens,
Sand and beach balls,
Your contact lens,
Apples and pears,
The TV and teddy bears,
Imagine if objects could speak...

Abigail Poole (12)
Kingsbury School, Kingsbury

My Reality TV Show...

If I had my own reality TV show
It would show all my friends
If I had my own reality TV show
There would be a lot of exciting bends
If I had my own reality TV show
It would show a lot of schools
I would rather be at the mall
If I had my own reality TV show
I would look as white as a ghost
In fact, I would be mistaken for a ghost!

Charlotte Howard (12)
Kingsbury School, Kingsbury

If I Was Homeless!

If I was homeless I would feel a lot of things
They would be
Unhappy
Lonely
Scared!

If I was homeless I would be in danger
This is why
Diseases
Traffic
Hunger!

If I was homeless I would have nothing
No water
No shelter
No food!

Rhianna Woolford (13)
Kingsbury School, Kingsbury

Feel Your Dreams

Imagine if your dreams came true
Be able to see the things you thought were impossible
Be able to feel the clouds
Be able to hear the birds tweeting in the glaring sun
Be able to smell the fresh blossom from the flowers
Be able to taste the fresh air.

Brandon Lewis (12)
Kingsbury School, Kingsbury

What If Objects Spoke?

What was that?
At the morning
Did that chair just speak?
Every object just spoke.
I hear them,
Do they know?
Maybe I should speak back?
Do they hear me?
Am I the only one
Who can hear them?
That man
In the corner
Just spoke to that wall.
What is the world now?
Is this the end of human life?

Aaron Lea (13)
Leyland St Mary's Catholic High School, Leyland

Imagine

Imagine a world where our greatest fears come to life,
Demons and spiders the size of a house!
And we are the size of a mouse,
Yet the creatures were scared of us.

Imagine a place full of light and joy,
Yet you stare into a mirror,
And see a world of pain,
Misery, and no matter how much you want to help someone,
Yourself stops you.

Imagine that you can fly, but can't get down.
Imagine that you are invisible, yet nobody notices.
Imagine that you were a monster, but not truly evil.
Imagine that...

Imagine crying, yet feeling happy,
Feeling sad and laughing.

Imagine an island that is desolate,
No,
Stop imagining,
You're on an island that is desolate,
Because everyone else is invisible,
Stop imagining,
The people appear, they are crying,
Stop imagining,

They are happy, you see a spider run along,
Yet you're not scared, you're happy,

Imagine that, you were the hero and the villain,
Created and destroyed worlds,
But you are both, you know that,
Imagine that...

Roxanne Parsons (13)
Manchester Communication Academy, Harpurhey

The Eye

Imagine.
You feel an unstoppable force tying you down,
Vortexes swirling around.
Light cowers as if shy,
Hiding behind the devoid eye.
Nothingness remains,
A silent voice.
Time stands still.
Out of choice.

You do not die,
But do not exist.
For now, you cannot resist.
Your mortal body strained,

You are being drained.

Jan Halas (13)
Manchester Communication Academy, Harpurhey

If The World Was Made Of Food

W hat would happen if the world was made of food?
O ur stomachs would be full?
R elaxing in a tub of warm cheese dip?
L etting global warming destroy this wonderful world - food will never taste the same again.
D estruction, we might end up with nothing at all, floating off into space with greed to blame.

O r would we use food as material like we use wood, metal and fabric?
F or if we eat the Earth's products that are for building with and build with food that is for eating

F ood and material would be swapped and
O verall, we wouldn't know the difference
O ur lovely little world would be like it is now and we would be imagining a world where we actually eat food!
D o you prefer this delicious world to the one we are living in now? How do we know we are living normally? Aliens might live on a planet of food and not know any different...

Louise Gould (12)
Oakwood School, Horley

Love Yourself

I'm on the stage, I see the purple ocean, I love it, I do, but I hope it'll let me go soon
Cameras flashing non-stop, how am I not blind?
The pain from the Twitter comments, can't people be kind?

I'm grateful for ARMY
Sometimes they calm me
If I wasn't me what would I be?
They all love me, now I see
But why is it one comment upsets me?
All those people cheering me on
And one person's comment lingers on

Treated badly by everyone because we're different
This society is clueless
Teaching people to love themselves

Practising over ten hours a day
Goes to show why I have back pain
My voice hurts, I sing too much
I nearly collapse at the concerts

Fans only see the happy side of us
ARMY sees both sides, happy, sad, good and bad

The contract signed for fourteen years of life
Keeps me lonely all the time

We're outcast by society
People use ARMY and me
A Grammy nomination, which we worked hard for
They didn't want to nominate us, they did it for the views, it's all a ruse

Called a pig in every Tweet, I'm human still, can't you see?

Brothers who protect me and an ARMY of people behind me
What more could I want?

Maddie Pelling (13)
Oakwood School, Horley

Clover

I'm the ying-yang, where everything good will follow with bad.
Where there is hope, there is despair.
Everything I do will affect the next.
What will come next?
My undying burden will always be a shadow,
Looming over me like a veil.

Is everything set in stone?
Or will every action gamble each outcome?
May Lady Luck grace me with her radiating presence.
Her golden luck, the purest of its kind.
But with mine, I'm barely clutching on, barely.
Cautious of my every move; others shouldn't
Bare the burden of my 'talent' alongside me.

Drowning in my deprecating thoughts.
Is my so-called luck worthy to be deemed as a talent?
They say I'm a freak.
I'm like a roulette machine, unpredictable to a normal person.
I'm smiling, then I'm in hysterics.

Was meeting them fate?
Was meeting him part of my twisted luck?
Can hope save me for any longer?
Dwelling in an endless loop of despair.

That is how my life will play out.
Imagine having the ultimate luck.
That's... me.

Emily Vo (13)
Oakwood School, Horley

The Sorrow In The Trenches

I am standing in the trenches, my heart racing
Me facing my biggest fear
Holding a large shotgun
It is not fun
Comrades falling down like bombs full of blood
And the trenches start to flood
Blood sprayed like a lawn sprinkler
It sprays all over my uniform
It stains and it is pain
The look in their eyes of innocence haunts me
Because thousands of flies surround their corpses
We did not get a choice
We lost our voice
Blood drips like an endless supply of water
And people lost their legs and got shorter
Suddenly *bang, bang, bang*
Three bullets go through my best friend
He did not know it was the end
Suddenly sadness turns to anger
I run across no man's land
They fall down like ragdolls
It scars me for life
Now I hold my British Army knife

My funeral shall come with peace
I beg to be buried next to my friend that has fallen
But now remember we fought for the life you live today
I see the light from above
I am coming, my old friend
To regain my pride.

Lucy Green (12)
Oakwood School, Horley

Imagine If I Was Immortal

Imagine if I was immortal
So many things I could see
Maybe I could stay 12
And continue being me

Imagine what people would look like
A thousand years from now
Will they have metal heads
Or will they get rid of the word 'how'?

Imagine if I was immortal
I would watch people I love die
Is it really worth being immortal
To tell them forever goodbye?

Imagine what the world would look like
A thousand years from now
Will the Earth still be spherical
Or will it be shaped like a piece of dough?

Imagine if I was immortal
I could finally travel to space
I would maybe own a robot
Or have an unbreakable face

Imagine what I would look like
A thousand years from now
Will I be a high-tech cyborg
Or will I look the same as now?

Tejas Bhat (12)
Oakwood School, Horley

A Perfect Place

I live in a world of fuss
Sometimes sitting on a bus
Sometimes sailing, always trailing
We live in a world of fuss

I'll close my ears, I'll close my eyes
I won't see a world of fuss

A forest, a wood, this is good
This isn't a world of fuss

In the middle of the forest, in the middle of the wood
This is what I'll find

A place, a house, a cabin, a hut
This world can never be cut
Be killed, ruined, destroyed, remade

Inside, inside what I will find
Will blow, will blow your mind

Never a lock, never a clock
Never to stop, never to rot

This place was joy
This place was rest
This place was the best

However sad
However mad
I must return to the world of fuss.

Owen Dwyer (13)
Oakwood School, Horley

Computer Game

C onducted by the player
O r are we avatars in a computer game?
M ysteries unsolved
P layed by a person or thing I don't know
U nder control, not making my own choices
T he thought scares me
E at, sleep, school, repeat
R eady Player One

G ot to go to my game, it has been switched on
A wesome fun
M agical adventures
E at, sleep, school, repeat

A n avatar, they could have done better
V ision of the perfect avatar
A gain and again, I run, walk and talk
T he truth, I was controlled by the player
A ctually, it is not that bad
R eady Player One.

Louis Greenall (13)
Oakwood School, Horley

The Orphanage

There are 31 of us here,
Today our brother is going to leave us.
Mum tells us this is an orphanage,
We all believe her.

The potato-like drawings are sat on the wall,
Grinning at us with poorly-placed faces.
Mum leaves us with our brother,
And a tense silence falls across the house.

I creep out of the door like a stealthy fox,
My mind a ball of curiosity waiting for a glimpse of freedom.
We've never left the house,
We've never dared go near the gate.

As I enter the gate,
A wave of dread and fear washes over me.
Our brother is on the floor,
Like a fish that couldn't get to water.

Lucy Duarte (13)
Oakwood School, Horley

Imagine You Can See The Future

Imagine you could see the future
If there was peace or torture
The possibilities could be endless
If you were smart or practically headless

Imagine you could create the future
If you could build any structure
Or perhaps you could create any structure
So strong with infinite features

Imagine you could change the future
Take anything or anyone out of capture
Now would it change the culture
Or would it provide more treasure?

Imagine you could save the future
Would you pick your family or would you pick nature?
What if the future is strange?
How far can you see, what is the range?

Sean Anyaogu (13)
Oakwood School, Horley

Imagine If We Lived In A Science-Fiction World

Imagine if we lived in a science-fiction world
Where we could drive and fly hovercars
Roads wouldn't be needed anymore
And accidents wouldn't happen again
Tall buildings and skyscrapers would tower over us
We would send messages by hologram
People would use hoverboards to fly around for fun
Robots could help us with our cooking and cleaning
Our deliveries would be done by drones
Everything would be like a computer
This whole world could be built on a different planet
And animals could live their life on Earth
And get their home back
So imagine if we lived there
In a science-fiction world.

Eldad-Leonard Soreata (12)
Oakwood School, Horley

The Orphan

As I pulled up my duvet, yawning
I thought to myself *I'll just wait till morning.*
All the others asleep at last,
Trying not to think of my horrific past.
My only friend was the man on the moon,
But even sometimes he would go away too.
But that night as I closed my eyes I saw a shadow flying high,
He came to me with the sweetest smile and told me he wanted to talk for a while.

We talked and chatted as darkness passed,
I thought to myself *hmm, this night has gone fast.*
He handed me a locket so I slipped it into my pocket
As the morning sun rose at last...

Abigail Killick (12)
Oakwood School, Horley

Imagine If They Knew The Real You

Imagine if they knew the real you
How easy and how hard you've had it
All the sleepless nights
Imagine if they knew
Imagine if they were like you
You hoped you were normal
No one is
Imagine if everyone was perfect
What is perfection?
Having an amazing body?
Having amazing grades?
Having money?
It doesn't matter, anyone is perfect
Imagine if people thought you were perfect
When you thought you were abnormal
People will either be nice to you or criticise you
Whether they know the real you
Imagine if they knew the real you.

Ayesha Zaman (13)
Oakwood School, Horley

When She Was Five

When she was 5
She once said
"I can fly"
While jumping off her bed

When she was 8
She said
"I lost my two front teeth"
When she got home from school

When she was 11
She said
"I'm starting my SATs"
Her anxiety crawling all over

When she was 13
She said
"I'm okay"
Pulling her sleeves over her wrists

Now she's 15
Her last words were
"I can fly"
While jumping off the bridge

Does anyone even care?
Was I needed?

Jasmine Keane (13)
Oakwood School, Horley

Trapped In My Head

T he devil's here
R unning around inside my head
A nger fills me up
P eople surround me
P raying for more
E vil is coming
D ying to know what's inside

I ncomplete, I still wonder
N obody around to help

M y head spinning round and round
Y oung to old, old to young

H ell is approaching me
E ven though I yell "Stop!"
A ll my questions have been answered
D ad? Is that you?

Oldriska Dickson (13)
Oakwood School, Horley

Imagine If You Were Invisible

Imagine if you were invisible,
Would it be as good as you think?
You could do what you want,
Yet you would be alone.
No one cares about you,
Because to them, you are not there.
Your mind takes over,
Flooded with thoughts.
Why am I invisible?
You can run from everything else,
'Cause you're invisible.
But how can you run from what's inside your head?
You're invisible,
Taking strolls wherever you go,
Trying to take your mind off things.
Imagine if you weren't invisible.

Holly-Ruby Jackson (13)
Oakwood School, Horley

Loneliness

Imagine if you had no friends and family...
What would you do?
You would be very lonely
Really lonely
Extremely lonely
Imagine if you were alone all your life...
Who would you speak to?
Who would you do stuff with?
How would you cope with life?
Imagine if you had no one to speak to
How would you deal with your problems?
Who would you go to?
Imagine if you had no friends and family
How would you live?
What would you do?
You would be very lonely...

Ellie-Marie Burchell (12)
Oakwood School, Horley

The Old House

T rees surround the house like a jungle
H urry up before the dream ends
E verything is dead

O minous music grows
L isten as the house screams
D arkness suddenly everywhere

H urry! It's coming to an end
O ut around the house is nothingness
U nder the house is another world
S omewhere, someone will make it real
E verything is dead.

Zara McKee (13)
Oakwood School, Horley

Imagine If...

Imagine if you could fly!
What would you do?
Would you get bored?
Would you do tricks?

Imagine if you could teleport!
What would you do?
Would you steal?
Would you enjoy it?

Imagine if you could turn invisible!
What would you do?
Would you commit crime?
Would you like it?

Imagine a superpower!
What would it be?
How much would you use it?
Would you enjoy using it?

Harry McMillan (13)
Oakwood School, Horley

The Trench

Can you imagine storming over the trench?
Not even knowing what your future holds,
You can only imagine what could happen,
Until it happens,
You can see your comrades falling and dying,
You can see them even crying,
You'd think they'd prepare you for the horrors,
But they don't, they leave your mind weak,
All you hear is crying, screaming, explosions,
Now can you imagine storming over the trench?

Daniel Youd (13)
Oakwood School, Horley

Imagine In Heaven

Imagine you went to Heaven...
The light at the end of the tunnel
The air would be fresh
The sky would be blue
The sun would be a spotlight
Imagine it was a dream

Imagine the pain went away...
The grief, hurt and sorrow
The feeling of joy and tranquillity
The stars would shine
The angels would fly
Imagine seeing the future

Dream, believe, create, succeed
Imagine

Leah Pattemore (13)
Oakwood School, Horley

Caveman Period

C ool tools
A dventurous caves with no light
V ery hard
E very day was painful
M esolithic period
A nd the
N eolithic period

P alaeolithic period
E mpty caves with fur coats
R ead the flames to cook the food
I nvent new tools to help
O ops, that must have hurt
D o well, my grunting friends.

Samuel Pannell (13)
Oakwood School, Horley

What If...

What if this is my world
And everyone's just living in it?
What if I can control everyone?
What if I can cheat the world
And make everything mine?
What would I do with all this power?
Can I make people disappear?
What if I'm not the only one capable of this power?
What if there are more like me out there?
What if I'm not alone?
What if I can be overridden...
Bang...

Zara Tyson-Davies (13)
Oakwood School, Horley

Imagine If...

Imagine if you could be invisible,
What would you do with that?

Imagine if you could be immortal,
What would you do with your life?

Imagine if you could see into the future,
Wouldn't you be scared?

Imagine if you had one wish,
What would you wish for, wealth or friends?

Imagine if kids ruled the world,
What would they do?
Would you be worried?

Alex Azoicai (13)
Oakwood School, Horley

The Main Character

Imagine you became the main character in your favourite
TV show,
As you are sitting down watching
The screen pauses
As the screen gets closer and closer
All you see is black
You wake up and you are in
Your favourite TV show
Is this reality or is this zeros and ones?
You sit there thinking
What do I do?
Imagine if you became the main character in your favourite
TV show.

Cohen Masters (13)
Oakwood School, Horley

Imagine If You Were Immortal

Imagine if you were immortal,
You could kill yourself a million different ways
And see what hurts the most,
There'd be nothing to be scared of anymore.

You could do whatever you wanted,
Plane diving with no parachute,
Or jump across buildings with no hesitation.

You could live forever and see what the future holds,
Imagine if you were immortal.

Grace Clarke (13)
Oakwood School, Horley

If I Could Fly

Imagine if I could fly
How much different it would be in the sky
I could see the world's largest crimes
Just by sweeping over high
I could fly over seas
And swim with the clouds
If only I could fly
I could be friends with the birds
The buildings below would be blurred
I'd never get bored
And I could travel abroad
Oh, if only I could fly.

Lara Symonds (12)
Oakwood School, Horley

Imagine If You Could Go Back In Time

Imagine if you could go back to any time in the past
To the dinosaurs perhaps
Or the first-ever maps
Even the Egyptians with their pyramids
And the Vikings with their spears

Imagine going back in time
To any special place in your heart
Or a memory bringing you back to the past
Back to the days before now
Or with the ghosts somehow.

Charlotte Crofts (12)
Oakwood School, Horley

Back To Life

Imagine you could bring someone back from the dead,
Would you bring someone famous
Or an old friend?
Would you bring a childhood pet
Or someone on TV you've never met?
Would you give life to someone who did great
Or would they rather wait?
Would you bring someone who died too soon
Or maybe people who went to the moon?

Connie Young (13)
Oakwood School, Horley

Imagine I Could Change History

I magine if I could change history
M exico would have no border
A fghanistan wouldn't have been bombed
G ermany wouldn't have fought us
I magine what life would be like
N ew technology could have been created earlier
E arth would not be the same.

Henry Duncan (13)
Oakwood School, Horley

Decaying

My fingers brush against the flower,
The scratches indicate my power,
Petals sprinkle into dust,
All around me I feel a gust,
The tears stream down my face,
As I wish I could feel their warm embrace,
I look back to see,
The world fading beside me,
I'm sorry...

Sophia Dues (12)
Oakwood School, Horley

Just Imagine If

Imagine if you were cloned,
Imagine if there was double trouble,
But imagine if there was double love,
Imagine if there was double the arguments,
But imagine if there was double laughter,
Imagine if there was double the grief,
But overall, imagine there was double of you!

Leah Branton (12)
Oakwood School, Horley

Invisible

Imagine if you were invisible
No one will notice you
Imagine a world where everyone thinks you're dead
Because your life would be invisible
No one will ever notice you
Imagine if you were invisible.

Harley Greenhalgh (13)
Oakwood School, Horley

Imagine That

So imagine this, you were relaxed,
You were forced to watch this fake be you,
But it isn't you, instead you were copied and erased,
No one would know,
They couldn't tell,
Maybe they didn't care,
They loved this replica more,
You hated this but it didn't care,
Perhaps it saw you in the mirror,
It laughed,
While it taunted you,
Maybe, just maybe it knew already,
You didn't know and it laughed to itself,
Even you fell for its ploy,
You were just a joke,
It got you locked up,
Imagine that, funny isn't it?

Luke Kierans (12)
Rudheath Senior Academy, Rudheath

The Reality Of It

The reality of it is that I have no privacy,
Cameras and people follow me around desperately,
Trying to keep up with me, trying to 'keep fit',
That is the reality of it.

The reality of it is my life is a joke,
People laugh on their sofas, drinking coke,
Telling me in the comments that my bed hair looks 'lit',
That is the reality of it.

The reality of it is that people hate me,
People hurt me, shame me,
Call me names, from someone named Kit?!
This is the reality of it.

Melissa Coppock (11)
Rudheath Senior Academy, Rudheath

The Individual

Imagine if you were the only individual on Earth
The only individual that could read minds
The individual who could time travel back to 100BC
The only one who could hear animals talk
And understand a bird squawk
Imagine if you could fly
It would feel like you would not die
Imagine if you could change history
Then your life may be a mystery
What if you never died and were immortal?
Then you could travel through a portal
If every dream came true
What if Napoleon won at Waterloo?

Lewis Marshall (12)
Rudheath Senior Academy, Rudheath

What Can You Imagine?

I magine
M agic
A wesome
G lorious
I ncredible
N aughty
E nglish.

Imagine
When you imagine you can be
Magic, awesome, glorious, incredible, naughty and English.
You can speak any language,
Imagine whatever you like,
Do awesome things,
Have a glorious life,
Be an incredible person
Or be the naughtiest child.
This is your story,
Be who you like.

Erica Bowden (12)
Rudheath Senior Academy, Rudheath

I Woke Up Famous

If my dreams came true I would focus a lot to make people happy, to win every football game.
Imagine if my dreams came true...
I just hope one day I wake up famous,
Imagine if one day I woke up and Bruno Fernandes congratulated me for getting a scholarship for Manchester United.
Imagine if my first game I got the winning goal.
I wake up and... oh my!
I have finally woken up famous,
I am finally known for what I like.

Miley Heath (11)
Rudheath Senior Academy, Rudheath

Forever

Alone in the world,
No one else left.
As time has passed
Everyone you know has gone.
As you wander forever,
Never ageing,
Never changing.

You remember the good times,
Unable to go back.
If only you weren't different,
In the way you are now.
Never able to join them,
In an endless sleep.
Not in endless life.

Luke Wilkinson (12)
Rudheath Senior Academy, Rudheath

COVID-19

COVID, COVID, COVID,
Has taken over our lives,
It's killing millions of people,
It has to stop!

COVID, COVID, COVID,
It's spreading like spider webs on a ceiling,
The virus, an army, lurking over countries,
If we don't do anything, it can put us to an end!
We need to work together!

Rhaghav Jevirajasingham (11)
Rudheath Senior Academy, Rudheath

Peace On Earth

Imagine if this world was rid of all evil,
That this world was at peace,
If wars would end and all conflicts would be resolved,
People would be free from the shadow of doubt,
No one would die by the hands of war,
If people would stop destroying the world,
With plastic,
We can change the flow of the tide.

Bella Harrop Dobson (11)
Rudheath Senior Academy, Rudheath

Herobrine

His eyes glow white in the night
He wields an iron pick
He terrorises villagers, his name is Herobrine
He is Notch's enemy, he is immortal
He has been deleted but when he wasn't he was unstoppable
If you see him in a world you are unlucky
Nothing, not even the void, can kill him
He is a demigod.

Dylan Lishman (11)
Rudheath Senior Academy, Rudheath

Imagine No WWI

Imagine if World War I never happened
Imagine if nobody died from gas in agony
People dying being strapped to their bed from the pain
Humans being treated like animals
Soldiers in hospital from shellshock (PTSD).

Grace Foster (11)
Rudheath Senior Academy, Rudheath

Imagine Being Immortal

Imagine being immortal,
Watching the world go by, watching friends age,
Never being able to die,
All that power,
Never another day off being ill, bleeding or in pain,
It would be immaculate.

Max Kimber (12)
Rudheath Senior Academy, Rudheath

A Life Without Crime

Punched, kicked, stabbed, beaten,
How would you feel if this was how you were treated?
There's no need to run, there's no need to hide;
In the real world, you would be frightened for your life.
Just imagine, imagine a life without crime,
No need to look behind in the middle of the night.
No need to clutch your purse when someone walks by.
Just imagine, imagine a life without crime,
A life on social media, not being terrorised.
Not using school as an escape, not trying to keep yourself awake,
No passing out because of stress 'cause you have too much on your plate.
Just imagine, imagine a life without crime,
No funeral for your family 'cause someone else decided it's their time.
Not being afraid to wear certain clothes 'cause you might attract unwanted attention,
Not being afraid to mention what might cause moral deterioration.
Just imagine, imagine a life without crime,
Our world would be at peace and not just a short-term paradise.

Mica Chaplin
Saint John Bosco College, Battersea

Imagine If Humans Were Extinct

Who would be doing all the jobs
To help the animals left on the land?
When pets are stuck at home and humans are nowhere to be found?
With the crying pets suffering from starvation
While feeling like they are below the ground.
Only if humans were about.
Who would fix the running kitchen taps overflowing the town?
The buildings collapsing from tall clouds.
The mysterious creatures crawling around,
To find a way of survival.
However,
There are many positives to humans not being around too.
The pollution cases would be extremely low,
As the environment would come back healthy to say hello!
The world would be recreated by the animals around the world,
As it is the animals who are always unconcerned.
The world would be at peace for once,
As the animals like their lives of luxury without any fuss.

Taleigha-Shae Harris Hines (11)
Saint John Bosco College, Battersea

They Said That History Is Set In Stone

They said that history is set in stone
But then she said: "What if it wasn't?
Imagine it, if it was me,
Who could have changed all that was written.
Imagine it, if it was me,
Who could have set those people free.
Imagine it, if I prevented all those wars,
If I had saved those blameless children!"
But then her face went blank and grey.
In a low voice she said: "I couldn't.
And after all, it's set in stone.
And after all, I can do nothing."
And suddenly her face lit up.
"Oh no, I can!" she exclaimed fastly.
"I cannot change what's set in stone,
But I can change what will be on it,
But I can change the world right now,
But I can change the future story."

Barb Kostina (14)
Saint John Bosco College, Battersea

At The End

Dark, black, mist, fog
The world is how it was before mankind came
The air is filled with smog
And the rivers are now lame

The land is covered with vegetation
No man to look after it
It is impossible to find any location
So the wildlife just split

A new continent formed of the plastic that humans produced
And more of the oceans are touched by plastic than humans ever had
The sea life has reduced
There are new animals walking widespread

Everything is dark above
But all is green below
Nothing is flying, not even a dove
The animals on the ground are starting to flow

But at the end
The world will say
That the people did lend
But they had the wrong day.

Luke Burt
Saint John Bosco College, Battersea

If Dreams Were Real

I magine if dreams
F ell from your mind and
D own into
R eality
E veryone has a dream to unfold and experience
A nd any dream can happen, from your
M ind to your
S oul, if you just believe in what you desire then it

W ill become your future, your new
E xquisite life, but you must
R emember that not
E veryone has a happy dream; some dreams are sad, some are filled with

R eally eccentric ideas, some are just
E verything from what you remember
A lthough you will eventually
L ose sight of the star you wished upon.

Rhiannon Pituc (11)
Saint John Bosco College, Battersea

If You Could Change History

Imagine if you could change history,
What would you do?
Would you invent the first pool?
Or stop the world war?
There are multiple things that can be done,
But what would you change, if you could only change one?
I would change the world war,
I would because learning it is quite a bore.
There are some interesting facts,
Just like how pigeons found their way back by following tracks.
That's what I would change, but what about you?
You could pick anything because there's many things to do.

Maluhky Stone
Saint John Bosco College, Battersea

Eternal

Imagine if humans were immortal,
Imagine if lives were eternal,
Imagine the infinite amount of birthdays,
Imagine the terrifying count of holidays,
Imagine all the hungry poor,
Imagine how many poor galore!
Imagine that, what a mess!
But humanity is not that confusing, bless!

Lorenzo Chetanneau
Saint John Bosco College, Battersea

24 Hours

Imagine you had 24 hours left
What would you do?
Who would you spend time with?
Where would you go?
Who would you miss?

Heryacos Habtamu
Saint John Bosco College, Battersea

Raise Us Up

Our world is at a divide,
But only truth can hide,
For our world to change
We can't live with our thoughts in a cage
Imagine if you could travel through time
It would be truly sublime!
The past is what *made* us alive
But it doesn't *keep* us alive
For us to make a stand
Even though protests are banned
This is just a challenge that we need to unhand!
Power can raise us up
But it can also tear us down
Equality is the light at the end of the tunnel
The shade is the struggle, and trouble
Democracy was and is delayed
But as a nation
Now we have to be the ones
The world remade...

Isla Bea Ford (13)
St Ives School, Higher Tregenna

Imagine If You Ceased To Exist

I magine if one day you woke up to find that no one knew who you were,
M emories are wiped clean of your existence,
A ny trace of who you once were vanished,
G one are the days they spent with you,
I mmediately, you are plunged into a world of solitude,
N o one to reminisce with about the fun times,
E verywhere you turn familiar faces strike you,

I magine if you were an outcast, unwanted and unloved,
F orever to be alone,

Y our whole sense of belonging snatched away,
O nly you know what you were like so many years ago,
U nderstanding that you are alone has never been harder,

C omfortless, crushed and crestfallen,
E nraged and envious,
A sking yourself, "Why me?"
S hunned by all around
E motion starts to cloud your judgement
D espair overwhelms you,

T he fear of becoming someone else envelops you,
O nly then do you see how your emotions are taking advantage of you,

- **E** choes of your past life try to consume you,
- **X** -rays couldn't diagnose your pain,
- **I** magine if no one knew the true you,
- **S** hakingly, wondering, *does anyone remember me?*
- **T** his was the time you were forgotten...

Evie Stattkus (13)
St Ives School, Higher Tregenna

Imagine If

Imagine if everyone was equal,
Imagine if you could change history,
Imagine if you were in charge,
Imagine if you were them.

Why do we discriminate?
Because of prejudice.
We are the root of the problem;
Our opinions are the root of the problem.

Imagine if everyone was equal,
Imagine if you could change history,
Imagine if you were in charge,
Imagine if you were them...

We are all responsible for our actions,
We are responsible for society's actions
And as a society, we need to work together,
Work together to end discrimination in our community...

Danielle Fox (13)
St Ives School, Higher Tregenna

Her-Story

Imagine if you could change history...
To her-story.
Imagine the world reversed
Just imagine.

Women vote, men don't,
Women work and bring in the money.
Women drive the expensive cars,
Women are the head of the house.

Men do the housework; look after the kids,
Men fight for their rights.
Men get paid less for the same job as women.
Men will learn how hard it is to 'be a woman'.

Women wear comfortable trousers,
While men wear ill-fitting dresses.
History is her-story
And we can change it.

Rowan Hodder (13) & Freya Baker (13)
St Ives School, Higher Tregenna

Imagine... No COVID!

Imagine a world with no Coronavirus,
Oh, how happy that would be,
All the places we could go to,
And the people we could see.
No more singing 'Happy Birthday'
Each time we wash our hands.
I'd rather be down on the beach
With my toes buried in the sand.
Face masks could be thrown away,
A sign that we are free
For every time I wore that thing
It made me want to scream!
This is what I can imagine
For our world today
A place where the fear is no more
And happiness is here to stay.

Fearne Slade (13)
St Ives School, Higher Tregenna

In The Deep Blue

Imagine you could swim like a fish
What wonderful things you would see
Jumping with dolphins in St Ives bay
Swimming with seals at Godrevy
Hiding in seaweed with the starfish at Prussia Cove
Nipping toes with crabs at St Michael's Mount
Dodging the local fisherman who drop their nets deep at sea
And floating bottles discarded in the sea
I wish I could swim like a fish
Hold my breath for hours at a time
I would love to live in the deep blue sea.

Esme Deacon (13)
St Ives School, Higher Tregenna

Freeze Time

Hustle and bustle,
Eternally forever and infinity,
The people and the trees,
The birds and the bees,
Frozen at will,
Infinite space and endless time,
Only one person for the reason and rhyme,
The Eves and the Adams,
The protons and the atoms,
All instantly still,
One person for it all and all for one person,
The ants and the stars, the ocean and the hot sun,
Would it be such a crime,
To freeze time?

Ollie Trevorrow (12)
St Ives School, Higher Tregenna

A Place

Imagine a place,
Where men and women were treated as equals,
Whatever the race,
But there is another sequel.
Have you actually noticed the difference in pay?
The amount men get,
If it was the same people would shout yay!
It's almost a bet!

Imagine if you could change the old times,
But how about the new?
Isn't this just a crime?
Where could this world go? Where to?

Eva Fox (12)
St Ives School, Higher Tregenna

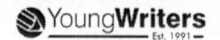

Imagine If...

Imagine if COVID-19 wasn't here

We wouldn't have to wear face masks
We wouldn't have to social distance
We wouldn't have to live under fear
We wouldn't lose our loved ones

Let's hope this happens
And that we can go back to normal.

Ella-May Haile (11)
St Ives School, Higher Tregenna

Life

I play
I paint
I watch movies until quite late
I eat
I sleep
I have fun
I lose fun
Lockdown is no fun and I miss the sun
It is just the way of life for now
Doing the same thing over and over... like I am on repeat.

Freya Scorer (12)
St Ives School, Higher Tregenna

Imagine If...

Imagine if you were the last person on Earth
Imagine if you were cloned
Imagine if objects could speak
Imagine all of this
It is very confusing
It is very weird
But we just have to deal with it,
As if it really did happen!

Flossy Calder (11)
St Ives School, Higher Tregenna

Unimaginable

Imagine, imagine, imagine...
a world that's like your dreams,
dreams that you thought would never come true.

Imagine, imagine, imagine...
those fairy tales coming true and your life becoming a fairy tale,
an old tale that was thought to not exist.

Imagine, imagine, imagine...
the worst happening that you thought was not going to happen
and you lose everything.

Imagine, imagine, imagine...
if you weren't human
and lived on another planet.

Imagine, imagine, imagine...
if everything you wished for
became true.

Imagine, imagine, imagine...
the endless possibilities to what you can imagine
I bet you can't though.

Because
doing that is unimaginable.

Angela Manjooran (12)
St John Fisher Catholic College, Newcastle

Believe...

In times of darkness, I said believe in light
You were financially broke, in a cruel money struggle
Working long hours, two jobs you had to juggle
Each penny counting towards your next meal
Which wasn't even a guarantee.
In this time of sorrow, I said believe in joy
But then it really hit in March 2020
The world shut down and schools, shops and streets were left empty,
Work from home, they said
But you weren't needed you were 'laid off' instead.
So you became jobless, and jobless meant homeless
But in this time of frustration, I said believe in patience
Even with very little food and no warm bed
Even though you struggled without a roof over your head,
We knew it would eventually came to an end,
Through perseverance, through strength,
And all of us coming together no matter,
Wherever, whenever or whoever
We slowly overcame the complications
And remember how I told you to believe
For in the power of belief lies hope for us all!

Aishah Mallah (12)
Waverley School, Bordesley Green East

No Gravity

Imagine if there was no gravity.
Everyone and everything would float around.
The apple would have missed Isaac Newton's head,
And he wouldn't have been known by the world.
Birds, bats and all the flying creatures,
Wouldn't be looked up to by those stuck on the ground.
Imagine all the things you could do.

You could then swim through the sky.
You could then touch the clouds,
And find out if they feel like soft pillows or like the air.

Water would be hard to get and drink,
As it would float as droplets through the air.
Your home would float away.
In stores, you would need to chase your shopping.

Imagine all that would happen.

Ayman Ali (12)
Waverley School, Bordesley Green East

The Chatty Life

Imagine objects could talk
Walking down the street
Saying hello to the lampost
And good morning to the flowers
And gossiping with the trees
And playing truth or dare with the fence
Being in your room, talking to the walls
Arguing with your alarm clock
And spilling your heart to your bed
Having a deep conversation with your teddy
And breaking up with your old shirt
It would be nice to have constant company
Like the world knows you
And everything has your back
There's always someone to chat with
Whether it's the sun in the morning
Or the moon in the night
Or perhaps even the stars
But we have to snap back to reality.

Aishah Saeed (12)
Waverley School, Bordesley Green East

Year Six

My time in Year Six,
Ironic but special,
Something but not a lot.
I didn't complete half of the book,
Due to a virus, that spread a lot...
There were many ups and downs
But I better turn my frown upside down.
Laughing and smiling was the thing I missed
When I looked outside and saw all the mist,
Reminding me: that's how my memory will be,
It's not very delightful, you see...
Devastated and angry for missing out on all the fun,
Cheering me up is my magnificent mum.
Teachers and friends, thank you for everything,
Entering at the bottom of my heart, you have everything.

Urooj Jamil (12)
Waverley School, Bordesley Green East

My Imagination

Imagine the world without light
Imagine walking in darkness
Imagine if darkness could take the day

Imagine how it could be if animals could talk
Imagine carnivores eating grass
Imagine herbivores hunting for flesh
And everything just being messy

Imagine men wearing skirts and dresses
Imagine women giving birth no more
Imagine people getting the freedom they've been craving
And the world favouring every being

Imagine the world with no roles
Imagine life with no learning
Imagine getting up and starting a day
In the middle of nowhere
Just imagine.

Rameesa Zamir (13)
Waverley School, Bordesley Green East

Just Imagine

Imagine meeting someone who understood even the deepest, darkest corners of your soul,
Imagine meeting someone who wanted to learn your past not to castigate you,
But to understand how you needed to be adored,
Imagine walking through the wind for the very first time,
For a dove to soar over a battlefield and see all war come to an end,
And for world hunger to be gratified as well,
Imagine the Earth populated by humans who have no capacity for people their own kind,
Imagine being in a world where no child knows what colour portrays what,
Red is now for blood, when it used to be love,
Just imagine...

Habiba Feryad (12)
Waverley School, Bordesley Green East

Imagination Turned To Reality

Imagine if there was peace in the world,
Imagine if there was no destitution in the land,
Imagine if there was no racism around the globe,
Imagine if we were all equal,
Just imagine,
Now use your imagination and try to make it a reality,
It would make our lives and everyone else's lives straight forward,
No more people being mercilessly shot,
No more blameless countries being bombed
And no more children and adults living on the streets,
Just imagine,
The future is ours to conquer,
As long as we have hope we can
Accomplish anything together.

Alisha Rahman (13)
Waverley School, Bordesley Green East

Lifelong

Some may say I am blessed with a long life,
I say I am most definitely cursed.
I live a pariah to society, in a hut down by the lake,
I have resided there for years,
Too many to count.
Each time I crawl out of my hovel,
Into the light,
I am punched by the memories of my past.
Every day I see people come and go,
And wait for my turn.
When will it be my turn?
Every person, every plant, everything I once knew,
Is gone.
They lived their lives to the fullest,
Yet I cannot, for my life is neverending.
A perpetual state of horror and pain.

Sameera Yasmin (14)
Waverley School, Bordesley Green East

Unequal World

Leaders always divide us into two,
But if I see it and you see it too,
Then why don't we raise our voice,
And why don't we make a choice
Between true and false?

Everyone should be loved,
No one should be shoved,
Everyone has struggles,
But everyone should have chuckles.

People fear change for one reason,
Change like the ending of a football season,
They fear that the nice things they own,
Can be stolen by different people that are unknown.
Bad people with no goals
Are actually nice people with good souls.

Hamna Iqbal (11)
Waverley School, Bordesley Green East

Am I A Monster?

I wake up with no memory of what happened
I reluctantly get up,
In confusion, I feel confused
My head feels like I got in a crash
When I finally get home to get a drink
I put my hand out
And the glass flies
Am I a monster?
I'm as powerful as a mobster
My life has changed completely
Should I flee?
Maybe I shouldn't, for any challenges to come I'm ready!
My knees are weak and arms are heavy
But what will my family think?
If they don't approve my heart will shrink
Maybe I am a monster...

Haris Qadir (12)
Waverley School, Bordesley Green East

I Have A Clone

I thought I was unique,
There was only one of me,
It is indescribable the technique they used to clone me.
I have a clone?

Why would they copy me?
There was no point at all,
Will they bring me to my fall?
I have a clone?

I see no reason,
Why they would commit this treason,
Why should this be shown?
I have a clone?

I am a clone,
There is more than one of me,
The world will be different,
Because there is more than one of me.

Abdullah Rashid (12)
Waverley School, Bordesley Green East

Dream In A Dream

I had just woken up
I was about to cry
I had a very bad nightmare
Wait, where was I?

I-I-I was at a train station
And I had a ticket in my hand
It said 9 and three quarters
It had just vanished into sand

I had a rush of emotions
Wizards and witches were around
I finally knew where I was
Therefore my heart began to pound

Running into the wall
My eyes began to close
I was back in my bed
When I started to doze.

Huriyyah Shah (12)
Waverley School, Bordesley Green East

Imagine If

Imagine if
Imagine if you could change the world
And with that one word
Everyone was treated equally

Imagine if you could go back in time
And teach people about love
And respect for others

Imagine if you could pause time
Many people would be saved
Instead of taking their last breath
And many families crying in pain

Imagine if
You were the last person on Earth
And seeing no one around you
What would you do?

Aamilah Hussain (12)
Waverley School, Bordesley Green East

Imagine, Imagine, Imagine

Imagine you were in Heaven
Would everyone be treated equally?
Would you not fight?
Would you make the correct choices?

Imagine you were the last person on Earth
Would you live in a mansion and live life
Or just use what you have then move on?

Imagine your dream came true
Would you be at the office or be chilling in your mansion?
But you could just help the poor and the homeless.

Kanz-Ul-Iman Choudhary (11)
Waverley School, Bordesley Green East

Imagine, Imagine, Imagine

Imagine if animals could talk
Imagine if you could pause time
Imagine a world without trees

Imagine, imagine, imagine

Imagine life was a reality show
Imagine being immortal
Imagine going back in time

Imagine, imagine, imagine

When we imagine we escape
We escape reality

Imagine not imagining
Life would be really dull
Imagine, imagine, imagine.

Malaika Muqaddas (14)
Waverley School, Bordesley Green East

Going Back In Time

Imagine if I could go back in time,
If I could stop crime,
Stop fights,
So there can finally be some light,
With all my might.

I can stop all pollution,
It would be my solution,
If I could go back in time
It's my time to shine,
I'll stop crime.

Thieving no more,
Burglary no more,
Imagine everything will be alright.

Faisa Haybe (11)
Waverley School, Bordesley Green East

Last To Live

Imagine being the last human on Earth...
Imagine how much that would make you worth
No more birth
Just you
Yes! You
And yet you wouldn't have a clue
The sky pale blue
So take your last steps
This could be your end...
Maybe not...
You could live for another 100 years
Without any fears
Of people...
Last to live.

Maleehah Rahman (12)
Waverley School, Bordesley Green East

Football

This game unites people together,
It's played as a team,
It's all about respect,
And having fun,

The beautiful game,
It fills me with joy,
You pass and you score,
And much more,

You play with passion,
And a smile on your face,
Everyone can play,
Any culture, religion and race.

Mohammed Raheel (14)
Waverley School, Bordesley Green East

How Does One Imagine?

How does one imagine?
Using our brains or minds?
Or maybe not,
Just an answer you must find,
Why does one imagine?
To think or protect
Thoughts from deep within
Maybe about a dolphin's fin?

Maybe
Or maybe?
How does one spell it?
Check a dictionary
Or just imagine it.

Farhan Hussain (11)
Waverley School, Bordesley Green East

Imagine, Imagine, Imagine

Imagine being alone
Imagine standing in front of a lion
Imagine becoming famous
Imagine seeing another world
Imagine having to lose someone
Imagine playing games all day
Imagine being lost
Imagine forgetting who you are
Imagine, imagine, imagine.

Yahya Mir (13)
Waverley School, Bordesley Green East

Step Boldly

Imagine the galaxy,
It is,
So beautiful,
When the night is clear.

But what about,

When the sky,
Isn't,
That clear,
Well...

Imagine the stars,
So bright,
And so beautiful.
Well they like to,
Play cricket,
They're the fielders.
Or sometimes they,
Go for a ball.
Or go for a swim,
In the darkness pool.
But they also,
Jump up and down,
In the Puddle of Gloom.

Or play catch,
With the sun,
And the moon.

But sometimes,
If you're lucky.
You'll find a gap,
In the clouds.
And,
If you take one bold step,
You might just find yourself,
On a roller coaster of imagination!

Step boldly!

Mia Wijesiri (10)
Whitehorse Manor Junior School, Thornton Heath

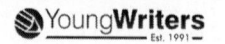

Water

Water is necessary,
Something most mortals know,
Some prefer to neglect it,
And let the water go

They leave on the tap,
Take long baths,
Leave the faucet trickling,
Give a drink to their flowers

More precious than gold,
The solution to my memoir,
H_2O should be concentrated,
And not be the origin of the struggle

Protect your water,
Don't let it fall,
It is our responsibility,
To keep liquid for everyone.

Gabriella Danso (10)
Whitehorse Manor Junior School, Thornton Heath

YoungWriters
Est. 1991

YOUNG WRITERS INFORMATION

We hope you have enjoyed reading this book – and that you will continue to in the coming years.

If you're a young writer who enjoys reading and creative writing, or the parent of an enthusiastic poet or story writer, do visit our website **www.youngwriters.co.uk**. Here you will find free competitions, workshops and games, as well as recommended reads, a poetry glossary and our blog. There's lots to keep budding writers motivated to write!

If you would like to order further copies of this book, or any of our other titles, then please give us a call or order via your online account.

Young Writers
Remus House
Coltsfoot Drive
Peterborough
PE2 9BF
(01733) 890066
info@youngwriters.co.uk

Join in the conversation!
Tips, news, giveaways and much more!

YoungWritersUK   @YoungWritersCW   @YoungWritersCW